Finance and A
for Non-Specialist Students

Alan Pizzey

formerly Principal L
Nottingham Busines
Nottingham Tren J

FINANCIAL TIMES
PITMAN PUBLISHING

FINANCIAL TIMES

MANAGEMENT

LONDON · SAN FRANCISCO
KUALA LUMPUR · JOHANNESBURG

Financial Times Management delivers the knowledge,
skills and understanding that enable students,
managers and organisations to achieve their ambitions,
whatever their needs, wherever they are.

London Office:
128 Long Acre, London WC2E 9AN
Tel: +44 (0)171 447 2000
Fax: +44 (0)171 240 5771
Website: www. ftmanagement.com

A Division of Financial Times Professional Limited

First published in Great Britain in 1998

© Financial Times Professional Limited 1998

The right of Alan Pizzey to be identified as Author
of this Work has been asserted by him in accordance
with the Copyright, Designs and Patents Act 1988.

ISBN 0 273 63020 2

British Library Cataloguing in Publications Data
A CIP catalogue record for this book can be obtained from the British Library

10 9 8 7 6 5 4 3 2 1

Typeset by Pantek Arts, Maidstone, Kent
Printed and bound in Great Britain by William Clowes Ltd, Beccles

The Publishers' policy is to use paper manufactured from sustainable forests.

Contents

Preface

The aim of this book is to provide a firm foundation in financial matters for the non-specialist student. Universities and Colleges teach a wide range of courses in business, economics, engineering, and other subjects for students who are working towards a managerial career in their chosen field. These students need a thorough introduction to the financial aspects of business, enabling them to understand financial statements produced for external or internal managerial purposes. Above all, however, the non-specialist student should be able to appreciate the effect of money on business operations, not only counting it but managing the finances of the entity with a view to taking part in the decision-making function. Accordingly, the depth to which the techniques and theory of accounting are treated in this book is carefully graduated for the non-specialist.

Finance and Accounting syllabuses for non-specialist students cover a wide range of topics, so this book is written to enable the teacher to select chapters which co-ordinate with a particular course. A study of the chapter synopses indicates that the book is written in three sections, to introduce accounting, to develop the principles of finance, and to apply financial information in a managerial context. Few study modules in finance or accounting will have sufficient study time to cover all three aspects, so the teacher is encouraged to be selective when designing a finance module to fit the requirements of particular students.

Teacher/Student contact time is at a premium these days so the chapters have been written to enable the student to work independently and to interact with the text by undertaking 'tasks' as each topic unfolds. Each chapter has discussion topics and practice questions to further illustrate the study material. Solutions to these questions are included to facilitate self-assessment by the student. The book is designed to introduce financial matters to students who are approaching this subject for the first time. The aims of each chapter are clearly established to guide students through the study material. A 'teachers, manual' is also available to focus attention on the major points which need to be developed from each chapter, with suggestions for lecture slides, and further questions with solutions for class work.

The book contains three appendices, which are included to underpin the learning activities of readers. They are:

(A) A synthesis exercise to build up from product costs and overhead expenses to a budgeted profit and loss account and balance sheet. This exercise helps students to understand the interplay of these statements with the cash budget. Some non-specialist finance courses use similar exercises as a means of assessment.

(B) A section on profit measurement on long-term contracts, including an example. This is a specialised area of accounting which is included for students on building and civil engineering courses who are studying a finance module.

(C) An examination paper with solutions. The paper contains six questions and is intended as a revision exercise to give question and answer practice in preparation for an examination.

This book has been written as a user-friendly text so that students who do not receive formal tuition can work through the material at their own pace. Terminology and principles are carefully explained and it is intended that the questions and solutions will clarify topics and engender a sense of confidence in students that they now understand the financial attributes of business.

Alan Pizzey, Ruddington
January 1998

1 The provision of financial information

The aims of this chapter are to enable students to:

- relate accountancy to the provision of useful financial information;
- appreciate the objectives of the corporate report;
- understand the wide spectrum of stakeholders who have an interest in that report; and
- explain the basic principles on which accounting statements rest.

ACCOUNTING FOR THE BUSINESS

Businesses and other organisations (e.g. hospitals, charities, local authorities) use resources that are under the control of managers. It is appropriate that the managers should report from time to time to those parties who have provided the resources, to inform them of the success of their operations, and the disposition of the resources entrusted to their care. In order to report, it is necessary to account for transactions (i.e. economic events such as sales, purchases, investments) and show their effect on the business during a stated period. Accounting has been defined as the process of identifying, measuring and communicating business information to facilitate judgements and decision making. To do this it covers many different activities and provides a service to a wide spectrum of interested parties both inside and outside the business. The elements of accounting which lead to the provision of financial information are as follows.

■ Accounting system

Setting up and operating an accounting system to recognise and record transactions implies that all economic events in the business, from the payment of wages to the purchase of a subsidiary company, are entered into the system, which is organised to minimise the possibility of resources being misused. Wages sheets, invoices, petty cash vouchers, bank paying-in slips and other prime documents are the means whereby transactions enter the system.

■ Classification and measurement

Transactions can be classified as creating assets or liabilities, costs or revenues, and these classifications can be further analysed into subgroups. Classification helps to sort out a great mass of transactions and reduce them to order.

TASK 1.1 How many subclassifications can you think of to analyse the costs of a business?

Solution

Your solution could include the following:

- material costs
- labour costs
- production overhead costs
- administration costs
- selling and marketing costs
- financial costs.

If classification produces a set of alternatives, so too does measurement. Judgement is needed to decide on the amount in money terms which will represent a transaction in the system. The value of an asset or the amount of a cost may vary according to the circumstances for which the figure is to be used. It is important to realise at an early stage that financial information is not precisely accurate, and that it may be the outcome of a series of assumptions or judgements, known as accounting policies.

TASK 1.2 A business own a factory building. How many ways can you think of to value the building?

Solution

Some alternatives might be:

- *historical value* (i.e. the amount paid when it was purchased five years ago);
- *replacement value* (i.e. the amount payable if it was bought today);
- *realisable value* (i.e. the amount receivable if it was sold today);
- *economic value* (i.e. the value of the profits to be made from the factory in the future).

■ Summarisation

Once all the transactions for a period have been recorded and classified they can be summarised into accounting statements. The profit and loss account sets cost against revenue to disclose a profit or loss for the period. The balance sheet lists the assets of the business and the claims against those assets from lenders and owners who have provided the funds used to pay for the assets. This discloses the financial position of the business. Cost statements also summarise a situation for managers entrusted with the resources used by a department.

▪ Communication and interpretation

The provision of financial information is not an end in itself. Accounting statements must be carefully drafted to disclose what users need to know, and what the law (the Companies Act 1985) says they have a right to know. The accountant can also interpret business activity by commenting on the statements, focusing attention on significant items, showing the relationship of one figure to another (e.g. net profit as a percentage of capital employed), and explaining the implications of the financial information for the policy and objectives of the business.

THE CORPORATE REPORT

This is the title of the document which a company, public or private, must produce each year to disclose its performance and financial position. Most companies produce an interim report at the halfway stage, but the annual report, usually published some months after the end of the financial year, is presented to the Annual General Meeting (AGM) for acceptance and confirmation by the shareholders who own the business. Such a report provides a significant opportunity for a public relations exercise and perhaps as much as half of the pages of the report are taken up by a chairman's statement, glossy photographs and other material in order to convince the shareholders that they are right to hold and retain their shares, and make further investments in the company.

The rest of the report concerns the financial statements, which are subject to an independent audit report confirming that they are 'true and fair'. These statements are as follows:

- ▪ *The directors' report*, which shows information prescribed by the Companies Act 1985 concerning directors, dividends, share capital, etc.
- ▪ *The profit and loss account*, which sets costs against revenue to disclose a profit or loss made during the period, and then shows how the surplus is appropriated to pay tax, and a dividend.
- ▪ *The balance sheet*, which analyses the assets as fixed (long-term) and current, and shows the claims against those assets by lenders and shareholders who have provided the funds to purchase them. This statement concerns one point in time – the period end.
- ▪ *The cash flow statement*, which analyses cash flowing in to and out of the business during the period.
- ▪ *The notes to the accounts*, which explain the figures in the accounting statements, such as an analysis of fixed assets, or debtors, or movements in shareholders' funds. A major note concerns the accounting policies covering the accounting methods, assumptions and judgements used to prepare the accounts.

■ *The auditor's report*, which confirms to the shareholders that the accounts presented to them by the directors who manage the company on their behalf show a true and fair view.

Some recent additions to the corporate report have been introduced to meet requirements of the Stock Exchange which, following the Cadbury Report, requires statements covering the corporate governance of the business.

■ The objectives of the corporate report

Corporate reporting is a costly exercise considering that a copy is sent to every shareholder, and it is expected that these costs will bring associated benefits. The objectives, however, are somewhat in conflict, and doubts remain as to whether the corporate report is worth the cost involved. The objectives of the report are as follows.

Statutory

The Companies Act stipulates that the directors who are elected by the shareholders to manage the business should report on their activities. Statute lays down the minimum amount of information to be disclosed and the format of the balance sheet and profit and loss account. The corporate report is a public document filed with the Registrar of Companies.

Stewardship

The financial information made available, accounts to shareholders for the actions of the directors in terms of profit made in the year, and assets owned at the end of the year. This is a backward-looking assessment commenting on recent past history, with directors reporting as 'stewards' to the owners of the business, whose funds they are elected to manage.

Decision usefulness

This objective is that the financial statements should provide shareholders with information that assists them with decisions which they need to take (i.e. to sell, hold, or buy shares in the business). Such decisions should be based on forward-looking information, so this objective is in conflict with stewardship, which reports on past activity. Directors are not willing to disclose their intentions in budgets, and auditors might find it difficult to report on such figures, so shareholders are left to update historical information with the aid of confident but unaudited public relations statements when they make their decisions.

Confirmatory

The market for investment funds is well served by information about companies as investments opportunities, but not all of this information is reliable. It stems from company announcements, stockbrokers' advice, and the financial columns of newspapers. Some information may be biased and some may be only rumour. The corporate report provides the investor with an opportunity to confirm this 'market information' against audited financial statements.

▪ Users of the corporate report

Every business has a wide spectrum of stakeholders with an interest in its operations, and the corporate report provides useful information to all these groups. It must be recognised, however, that the information needs of groups of users differ widely, and the corporate report is subject to considerable conflict to meet these disparate requirements. At the same time, many user groups do not pay for their information, since the cost of the corporate report is borne out profits which belong to the shareholders. The main users can be grouped together as follows.

Shareholders

The legal owners who have invested in the business by buying shares cannot easily be considered as a single group. An individual may hold a few shares, while an investment institution such as a pension fund may own as much as a five per cent stake in the company. Potential shareholders who are considering the purchase of shares, and especially other companies contemplating a take over bid, will also use the corporate report, but with varying degrees of financial sophistication. Some shareholders are interested only in the dividend to be paid, while others need to know about the 'quality' of profits (will they continue into the future), the disposition of assets, the ability of the business to survive and grow, and the risks involved with their investments.

Managers and employees

Most managers will know a great deal about that part of the business under their control, but comparatively little about other parts of the business. People who work for a company have invested their careers rather than their money, and they need an overview to inform them about company performance and the chances of continuing employment and promotion. Trades union representatives also have an interest in the performance of the business.

Lenders

Lenders can be divided into long-term or short-term lenders to the business, but they all have an interest in the security of their loans, and the risk that they will not be repaid. Some long-term loans may be secured on the fixed assets of the business (e.g. plant, property) with interest paid on the loan up to the date of repayment. Such lenders need to know whether the profit made is enough to cover the interest and whether the assets are sufficient security for their loans. Short-term lenders vary from banks which have advanced large amounts of overdraft finance, to trade creditors who need to be paid soon for goods supplied on credit terms. These lenders are interested in the short-term assets of the business (i.e. stocks and debtors) that will soon generate a cash flow from which they are to be repaid.

The Inland Revenue

The published accounts provide the starting point for the tax computation, which works from the accounting profit to the taxable profit on which corporation tax is levied. Some costs are not allowable for tax purposes and must be added back to the profit, while taxation allowances are then deducted. Depreciation is not a tax allowable expense so it is added back to profit, and then capital allowances calculated for the fixed assets are deducted.

Customers and competitors

Customers use financial statements to ensure that they are buying from a reputable business with sufficient resources to perform according to contract. This is particularly important when a subcontractor or component supplier is involved. Competitors use published financial statements to assess the profitability and financial status of rival firms. Competitors are particularly interested to see an analysis of the turnover of another business to compute market share, but managers are keen to preserve the confidentiality of some items, and thus disclose only the legal minimum of information. In some industries it is possible to organise an interfirm comparison scheme whereby accounting ratios computed from corporate reports are compared with the average for a similar group of companies as a measure of performance.

Analysts and advisors

This group comprises stockbrokers, financial advisers and columnists who are among the most financially sophisticated users of the corporate report. They are specialists in 'market information' and use the corporate report to check on other information they have gathered through various channels.

The corporate report has somewhat conflicting goals, and provides information for a wide spectrum of users with disparate levels of financial sophistication and quite different requirements so far as information is required. No single document can cater adequately for all these needs within the parameters of cost/benefit considerations and the needs of managers to preserve confidentiality.

TASK 1.3

As a supplier of raw materials, you sell £50 000 of goods to one customer each month, allowing payment three months after delivery. What items in the corporate report of your customer would be of interest to you?

Solution

Some points in the solution might be:

- the amount of liquid assets – cash and short-term investments in the balance sheet with which to pay the £150 000 you are owed (i.e. 3 months × £50 000);
- the claims of other creditors, including the bank overdraft and unpaid taxation, on the liquid resources of the business;

- the amount of debtors and stocks in the balance sheet which will turn into cash eventually;
- the volume of cash flow in the cash flow statement;
- a profit; remember that losses waste the resources of the business which will then no longer be available to make payment.

MANAGEMENT ACCOUNTING

The corporate report provides information to those outside the business, but management accounting is used to provide financial information that will assist managers with their tasks of planning, decision making, communicating, organising, and controlling the transactions of the business. Management accountants adopt a different attitude from the financial accountants who produce the corporate report, derived from the different situation in which they work. The major differences are as follows.

Users

The corporate report has a wide spectrum of users, but a management accounting statement is tailored to fit the needs of the managers involved, and is often limited to the operations under their control – a department. Management accounting must be cost effective, providing information which will enable managers to control operations, perhaps by a comparison of budgeted cost to actual cost, or will assist them in solving problems and deciding appropriately when alternatives present themselves.

Statutory requirements

The corporate report is confined within a set of disclosure rules contained in the Companies Act 1985, and further accounting rules (i.e. Financial Reporting Standards (FRSs) laid down by the accounting profession. There is no set format for a management accounting statement, which is drafted in a form that will be most helpful to the recipient. While the corporate report is a public document available for all to see, management accounting deals with matters which are confidential to the business.

Periodicity

The corporate report for the year looks back on what has taken place, and appears several months after the end of the period. Management accounting provides more immediate information, since managers cannot wait to learn of the success or failure of their activities and organise remedial action if necessary. The period covered by a management accounting statement might be a week, or a month, or a quarter, but to be of interest to forward-looking managers the statement must be completed very soon after the end of the accounting period. This creates a tension, since the need for speed in reporting is often achieved by forgoing accuracy, and the management accountant must establish tolerances with the managers to whom the information is provided.

Analysis

The corporate report gives an overview of the whole business, with comparative figures for the previous year, but management accounting analyses transactions to show the contribution made by the constituent parts to the overall profit. Management accounting can compare performance with a previous period, but it is more likely to make a comparison of actual with the budget or planned performance in order to identify remedial action required at an early stage.

Technique

Management accountants use the financial accounting system, but that is only a part of their activities. Forecasting and budgeting will need the skills of the mathematician and economist to deal with risk and uncertainty, while the application of behavioural theories assists when control reports are made. Above all management accounting is forward looking.

Audit

A further statutory requirement is that the corporate report should be subject to an audit in order to confirm the reliability of the statements submitted by the directors to the shareholders. With management accounting there is no such formal audit, but the system of internal control will build in checks and balances to ensure the reliability of the figures. The management accountant will need to explain to the recipient of the statement, the assumptions and techniques applied to produce forward-looking management information. The internal audit department, which checks the operation of the accounting system and protects the assets from misuse, is an important part of management accounting. Managerial information is expensive to produce and, accordingly, is subjected to a different type of audit based on cost/benefit principles, whereby the worth of financial information must be proved and its use optimised if its production is to be maintained.

THE CHARACTERISTICS OF USEFUL FINANCIAL INFORMATION

Whether in the corporate report, or as part of management accounting, the design and provision of financial information must conform to certain principles.

Relevance

The accountant must accept the discipline of selecting information that is of interest to the user. The statement gains focus by highlighting significant points, and adapts the format of the information to meet user needs. This characteristic is more important for management accounting than financial reporting, where statute prescribes what is to be disclosed and user needs are spread over a wide spectrum of stakeholders. Non-relevant information supplied to a manager may complicate performance evaluation or the issue on which a decision is to be made, and can lead to mistakes in the absence of clear focused thought.

Reliability

Financial information must be reliable if it is to be used with confidence. An audit report, verifying the system used and confirming the methods and assumptions applied, will increase user confidence. Accounts should be complete and free of bias, showing all aspects of the situation. There is a tension here between the need for relevant figures (e.g. the current value of property) and reliable figures, when valuation can produce widely different amounts for the same asset depending on the individual valuer and the method used.

Understandability

A useful financial statement will present its information as simply as possible and in a format which is easy to assimilate. A complicated mass of detail will confuse users, but the oversimplification of complex business affairs will not communicate adequately with users. As in the corporate report, a brief statement accentuating certain figures will need to be supported by notes to the accounts that give a more detailed explanation to those users who can appreciate further analysis.

Perspective

Financial information may be confusing to users unless it is set in context by the disclosure of 'comparative' figures. The corporate report always places last year's figures alongside current information. Good management accounting will show figures for the same month last year, or for the budget this month, or will quote costs as a percentage of the total, or per unit. The consistent use of accounting rules and assumptions enables comparison to be made with other firms, both within and outside a group of companies.

Timeliness

Information which is out of date has lost much of its usefulness for control, appraisal, or decision-making purposes. Good managers are by nature forward looking and thinking of the next set of transactions to be organised, so delayed cost information may be seen as an irritant rather than a cost-effective management tool.

THE BASIC PRINCIPLES ON WHICH ACCOUNTING STATEMENTS REST

Some assumptions are so fundamental to the accountant that it is assumed that they are followed when accounts are drafted, and a note to the accounts must warn users if this is not the case. There are *four* important principles which are enshrined in most financial information.

■ The going concern

When the accounts of a business are drafted it is assumed that the business is going to continue in operation in the future. Without this assumption, assets would have to be valued at what they would realise if sold, and this amount is very different from their 'book value' (i.e. historic cost less depreciation to date) or 'value to the business' (i.e. if they are held to be used in profit-making operations rather than for immediate sale). The auditor must be satisfied that the business is a going concern.

TASK 1.4 What items do you consider to be significant when judgement is exercised to test the going concern assumption for a business?

Solution

Some points worthy of consideration are as follows:

- ■ Short-term financial viability – Can the business pay its way in the future? Are its liquid resources (e.g. cash) insufficient to meet known liabilities, in which case trade creditors and the bank will no longer have confidence to lend short-term finance?
- ■ Capital structure – Has the business balanced its long-term capital requirements between owner and lenders, and can it recruit additional funds to finance future operations? Is profit large enough to give confidence to investors to risk their funds?
- ■ Competitive condition – Is the business efficient in terms of costs, and can it acquire sufficient materials, labour, and new plant to continue in the future?

■ Matching, or the 'accruals' principle

When a profit is measured it is important to match the cost of earning sales revenue with that revenue, so that cost and revenue represent the same goods and time period. The cost of goods purchased but not yet used is carried forward to next year as the closing stock, a short-term asset in the balance sheet. It would be wrong to charge the cost of materials not used against the revenue earned by the sale of other products.

■ Prudence, or 'conservatism'

Uncertainty exists in most business transactions until the deal is complete, so a prudent approach is needed to avoid counting a profit before the transaction is finalised. The accountant will select the lower asset value, or profit, when alternatives are available in order to avoid overstating a profit and paying a dividend out of a surplus which later proves to be illusory. This rule can be summarised as: 'Anticipate no profit and provide for all possible future losses'.

Matching prompts accountants to carry forward unused cost items as assets, but prudence demands that those assets are valued at realistic/conservative amounts.

Hence the rule for the valuation of stock in the balance sheet at the lower of cost or net realisable value, to take no profit made because stock values have increased since their purchase, but to account for any loss made if stocks are worth less than their cost at the balance sheet date.

Prudence can be misused by accountants who make provisions against profit in a good year to release in a bad year, thus smoothing out the fluctuation of business income and disclosing a false picture to users. Bias in accounts caused by understating asset value departs from the need for correct reliable figures.

■ Consistency

Judgement in the selection of appropriate values and methods to use when drafting financial statements is an essential part of accounting. Once the choice is made, the same method must be used in future years if comparability over time is to be achieved. To change methods in order to increase the profit disclosed is to introduce an unacceptable element of bias into the accounts. Change is only allowed to improve the true and fair view disclosed in the statements.

OTHER CONVENTIONS OF ACCOUNTING

Accounting principles depend for their authority on their acceptance by accountants as the best way to operate. Accordingly change is slow as the accounting profession reacts to new situations. Important principles are as follows:

■ *Objectivity* (as opposed to subjectivity), which seeks to verify the value accorded to transactions by evidence (an invoice), rather than by valuations which may be biased;
■ *Materiality*, which holds that unimportant items should not be allowed to confuse the message contained in a financial statement and need not thus be disclosed. Unfortunately, a good definition of what is 'material' has not yet been agreed;
■ *Substance over form* – a relatively new principle – suggests that the strict legal form of a transaction can be ignored if it impedes the disclosure of a true and fair view, and can be substituted by the economic substance or commercial effect of the transaction. If a company leases a machine from a bank, the asset belongs to the bank, and if the rentals are paid up to date then there is no amount owing. Thus the legal form of this situation is that no asset or liability exists in the company accounts at the balance sheet date. However, if, as part of the leasing contract, the company has a right to control the use of the machine throughout its working life, the machine may be considered as an asset of the company, rather than of the bank. If future rentals are agreed as payable by a contract, then they too should appear in the balance sheet as a long-term loan. In this and similar situations most accountants now agree that economic substance requires the balance sheet to show the asset and the liability.

CONCLUSION

In this chapter, we have demonstrated the great variety of financial information provided by organisations, and the very real differences between information for users outside the business and for managers. A further problem is the disparity of financial sophistication between user groups and the tensions which this places on providers of financial information. Statute and principles have evolved to ensure that a minimum of useful information is adequately presented, but inevitably, accounting statements cannot fully meet the needs of all users. Good accounting is not an end in itself, but must be judged on the usefulness of its product, and depends also for its value on the skill and judgement employed and on the methods selected for application when transactions are processed.

DISCUSSION TOPICS

Thirty-minute essay questions

1 'Accountancy is not only concerned with recording transactions, it provides a service to a wide spectrum of interested parties.' Discuss.

2 'Corporate reporting is a costly exercise, but the objectives of the exercise are far from clear.' Explain.

3 The information needs of the various groups of users of the corporate report vary widely. Who are these users and how far do their needs for financial information differ?

4 Relate the characteristics of useful financial information to the information needs of a manager.

2 The major accounting statements

OBJECTIVES

The aims of this chapter are to enable students to:

■ understand the format of the profit and loss account, and how it sets costs against revenue in order to measure the performance of the business;

■ understand the format of the balance sheet, and how it sets assets against liabilities in order to disclose the financial position of the business; and

■ discuss the meaning of the term 'profit' with reference to the maintenance of capital.

INTRODUCTION

The major accounting statements are the profit and loss account, the balance sheet, and the cash flow statement (CFS), which appear in the corporate report, and the budget, which is a management accounting statement. The CFS is covered in Chapter 7 and the budget in Chapter 15, so this chapter concentrates on the first two statements mentioned above. There is some argument amongst accountants as to which is the more important, but in fact they complement each other, to disclose the performance and the position of the business.

THE PROFIT AND LOSS ACCOUNT

This statement sets revenue earned during the period (£158 424 in the statement for Mansfield Brewery) against the costs incurred to earn that revenue, to disclose a surplus or deficit (a profit or loss for the period £20 839). The statement then shows how the profit made has been appropriated: part to pay tax (£5828); part to pay a dividend to the shareholders (£4561); and the remainder, which also belongs to the shareholders, to be retained in the business as part of the reserves to finance forthcoming activities (£10 450).

A profit and loss account drafted for managerial purposes will analyse the costs under many different headings, but in the corporate report the analysis discloses turnover *less* cost of sales (£106 116) in order to calculate the gross profit (£52 308), *less* operating expenses (£26 093) to calculate operating profit (£26 215) *less* finance charges (£5590) to calculate net profit before tax (£20 839). The operating expenses are selling and distribution costs, and administration expenses, (which are disclosed by Mansfield Brewery as part of note 2 to the accounts).

A further piece of analysis is to show the effect on profit of exceptional items such as windfall gains from the sale of assets (£214), or losses made by reorganisation, the closure of branches, or the sale of subsidiaries. These items are not part of normal trading and are shown separately to inform users. Where necessary, the profit and loss account down to finance charges will be analysed into separate columns for ongoing activities, discontinued activities and new acquisitions, again to inform users of the constituents of the profit figure. The earnings per share (23.15p) is the net profit after tax divided by the number of shares which have been issued. Note that the figures for the previous year are shown as a comparator.

TASK 2.1 Identify the figures mentioned in the section above on the profit and loss account of Mansfield Brewery plc for 1997. Figures are in £000's.

Profit and Loss Account for Mansfield Brewery plc for year ended 29 March 1997

	Notes	1997 £000	1996 £000
Turnover	1	158 424	146 881
Cost of sales		(106 116)	(100 266)
Gross profit		52 308	46 615
Other operating expenses	2	(26 093)	(22 641)
Operating profit	1	26 429	24 067
Surplus on disposal of properties		214	93
Profit on ordinary activities before interest		26 429	24 067
Finance charges	5	(5 590)	(5 622)
Profit on ordinary activities before taxation			
Trading profit		20 625	18 352
Surplus on disposal of properties		214	93
		20 839	18 445
Tax on profit on ordinary activities	6	(5 828)	(5 153)
Profit on ordinary activities after taxation		15 011	13 292
Dividends paid and proposed	7	(4 561)	(3 815)
Amount set aside to reserves	17	10 450	9 477
Earnings per share	8	23.15p	20.62p

ACCRUALS AND PREPAYMENTS

The matching concept stipulates that sales revenues for a year should be matched with the costs of producing the goods which have been sold. If 10 000 units are in stock at the beginning of the year, 50 000 are bought and 20 000 remain in stock at the end, then 40 000 have been sold and the cost of these units must be the cost of sales. For example:

	£	£
Sales		600 000
Opening stock 10 000 units	100 000	
plus Purchases 50 000 units	500 000	
	600 000	
less Closing stock 20 000 units	200 000	
Cost of sales 40 000 units		400 000
Gross profit		200 000

What if all the costs incurred are not recorded in the ledgers at the year end? Suppose 5000 units at £10 each have been received and are counted in closing stock, but the invoice has not yet arrived from the supplier on 31 December, the accounting date. The recorded figure for purchases must be increased by £50 000 in order to calculate the true cost of sales as £450 000. At the same time, the accounts record the fact that £50 000 is owed to the supplier as a current liability on the balance sheet. This adjustment brings recorded transactions into line with actual transactions and is called an *accrual*.

If invoices for electricity have been received up to 30 November, but power has been used in December, the amount to be accrued is the electricity cost for December which should be estimated, added to the recorded cost of electricity in the profit and loss account, and shown as a creditor in the balance sheet.

The opposite of an accrual is a *prepayment*, which occurs when the cost recorded in the ledgers is more than the cost incurred. If an insurance premium of £120 000 is paid in advance for the year on 1 September, then only £40 000 of the cost is incurred for the year ended on 31 December, and at that date the insurance company owes the business £80 000 of service. Thus the cost of £120 000 is reduced by £80 000 in the profit and loss account and a debtor of £80 000 is shown as a current asset in the balance sheet at 31 December. The cost of the year is adjusted to be matched with sales revenue of that year, and measures a true profit.

TASK 2.2

A business has paid rates on its premises of £4000 for the half-year April to September 19x1, £6000 for October 19x1 to March 19x2 and £6000 for April to September 19x2. Calculate the charge for rates in the profit and loss account for the year to 30 June 19x2 and the balance sheet debtor at that date.

Solution – Calculate in months

	£
July to September 19x1 £4000 × $\frac{3}{6}$ (three months)	2 000
October 19x1 to March 19x2 (six months)	6 000
April 19x2 to June 19x2 £6000 × $\frac{3}{6}$ (three months)	3 000
Cost for twelve months	11 000

The prepayment at 30 June 19–2 is:

$$£6000 \times \frac{3}{6} = £3000$$

as a current asset in the balance sheet.

TASK 2.3 A business has received three quarterly telephone bills for £1700, £1900 and £2100, but the invoice for the quarter to 31 December has not yet been received and entered in the ledger. The last quarter is estimated to have cost £2300. Calculate the telephone cost for the year to 31 December in the profit and loss account, and the creditor in the balance sheet at that date.

Solution

The telephone account in the ledger shows £5700 spent so far, but there is an accrual for the cost incurred but not yet recorded of £2300.

	£
Cost recorded (£1700 + £1900 + £2100)	5 700
add Accrual	2 300
Cost for year	8 000

The balance sheet will show as a current liability, the telephone company as a creditor owed £2300. When the bill is received in the next accounting period it cancels out this credit balance and will not therefore be part of the telephone cost for the next year. Thus the cost is matched to the period.

PROVISIONS AND RESERVES

A provision is an amount set aside out of profit to meet a known cost whose amount is not yet certain. Provisions are made as part of the prudence principle and to ensure a good match of costs against revenue.

Suppose customers owe £450 000 for goods received but not yet paid for, and this is the balance of debtors in the balance sheet on 31 December 19x1. No doubt most will pay what they owe within the next few months, but there is a possibility that one per cent of the money may not be received. This amount of £4500 is a cost of the year up to 31 December 19x1 but the amount is only an estimate, and the loss will be felt in 19x2 when the doubtful debtors do not pay.

Thus a provision for doubtful debts is made by charging the profit and loss account in 19x1 with £4500, and deducting £4500 from the debtor's in the balance sheet. When, therefore, the loss is incurred in 19x2 there is a provision to offset the amount, so that bad debts of 19x1 do not affect the profit of 19x2, unless the provision made was not sufficient to cover the cost.

If a machine is purchased in 19x1 for £10 000 and it is expected to have a useful economic life of five years, it seems fair to charge each of those years £2000 for the use of the machine, to match the cost to the revenue earned by the machine. The term *depreciation* is used for this amount, which is not certain but is a good estimate of the cost concerned. Thus £2000 will be charged against profit in 19x1 as a provision for depreciation which will also be shown in the balance sheet as a deduction from the asset – the machine, which will be shown as cost £10 000 less depreciation to date £2000, a net figure of £8000.

TASK 2.4   A company buys a vehicle for £20 000 which is expected to have a working life of four years, after which it will be worthless. Calculate the provision for depreciation charged against profit in the first year and show how the vehicle would appear in the balance sheet at the end of that year, and the next year.

Solution

Cost £20 000 ÷ 4 years = £5000 charged per annum to profit and loss account. The balance sheet will show the vehicle at cost *less* the amount of the provision to date:

	£
Fixed asset	
Vehicle at cost	20 000
less Provision for depreciation	5 000
Net book value	15 000

At the end of next year it will show:

	£
Fixed asset	
Vehicle at cost	20 000
less Provision for depreciation (2 years × £5000)	10 000
Net book value	10 000

This is a book value and may not correspond to the real value of the asset.

Now compare this solution with the *tangible assets* note of Mansfield Brewery plc shown below (p.19). Do not forget that provisions are always deducted from the assets on the balance sheet.

A reserve is an amount set aside as a matter of financial policy, *after* the profit is determined – it is not a cost. It shows users that the directors do not intend to distribute this part of the profit, but plan to use it to finance future operations. The reserve can be for a specific purpose (e.g. to build a new headquarters), or as a general reserve, sometimes merely termed *Unappropriated Profit* – (see the Mansfield Brewery balance sheet – £89 140). Other reserves are of a capital nature and will be dealt with as part of the balance sheet section below.

THE BALANCE SHEET

This is a statement as at a point in time, and as such shows the position of the business, by setting assets against liabilities and capital. All the assets in the business have been financed either by the shareholders' investment or by borrowings, so assets minus liabilities must equal capital. Expressed as A – L = C this is the 'accounting equation' and is derived from the balance sheet.

The format of the balance sheet can be expressed as the following formula:

Fixed assets + (current assets – current liabilities) – long-term liabilities
= Shareholders' funds

This corresponds to A – L = C, since the value of the assets *less* what is owed to others must belong to the legal owners – the shareholders.

An asset can be defined as an item which has a value and which is owned by a business. Value stems from the fact that the asset can be used in the business to earn a profit, or exchanged across the market for an amount of purchasing power. Ownership is now a less important part of the definition since, according to the principle of substance over form, it is control of the item rather than legal ownership that decides who should account for the asset. A more recent definition of an asset is that it is an item from which future economic benefits are expected to flow, and the right to those benefits belongs exclusively to, or can be controlled by, the business. A liability is an amount owed by the business, a borrowing to be repaid at some future time, but it can be defined as an obligation to transfer economic benefits as a result of past transactions.

■ Fixed assets

Fixed assets can be tangible (£233 809 in the statement for Mansfield Brewery), long-term investments (£24 398), or intangible, a classification which includes goodwill, brands, patent rights, and so forth. Investments and tangible assets are disclosed at cost, but if their value is subject to impairment they should be written down to a true value under the prudence concept. Tangible fixed assets such as land and buildings (£12 476 and £191 484 in the note to the accounts), and plant and vehicles (£29 849) are items held by the business for more than a year, and used to earn a profit. Depreciation spreads the cost of a fixed asset over the years of its useful economic life, so fixed assets are disclosed at cost *less* accumulated depreciation to date – the net book value.

The Mansfield Brewery Note 10 shows the total amount at the beginning of the year (£254 686), *plus* additions (£22 375), *less* disposals (£4071), in order to calculate the closing cost or valuation (£272 990). Similar analysis for depreciation gives the charge for the year (£6472) and the closing accumulated amount (£39 181). Cost (£272 990) *less* depreciation to date (£39 181) gives the net book value on the balance sheet (£233 809). The note analyses this total to classes of assets.

▪ Current assets

Current assets are items which are expected to be held for less than a year before they are turned back into cash. The Mansfield Brewery balance sheet shows stock (finished goods and materials for machines to work with) (£5226), debtors and prepayments (£15 994), mainly derived from trade credit given to customers, and cash itself (£3997). Note that the balance sheet also shows debtors due after more than one year (£6363) as a current asset. This item concerns trade debtors with extended trade credit, and is best disclosed with the other current assets rather than as a fixed asset.

TASK 2.5   Identify the figures mentioned in the balance sheet section on the balance sheet of Mansfield Brewery plc for 1997. Figures are in £000's.

Balance sheet for Mansfield Brewery plc as at 29 March 1997

	Notes	1997 £000	1996 £000
Fixed assets			
Tangible assets	10	233 809	220 496
Investments	11	24 398	23 764
		258 207	244 260
Current Assets			
Stocks	12	5 226	5 079
Debtors falling due within one year	13	15 994	12 780
Debtors falling due after more than one year	13	6 363	5 062
Cash at bank and in hand		3 997	3 100
		31 580	26 021
Creditors			
Amounts falling due within one year	14	(32 534)	(29 072)
Net current (liabilities)/assets		(954)	(3 051)
Total assets less current liabilities		257 253	241 209
Creditors			
Amounts falling due after more than one year	14	(85 645)	(81 501)
Provision for liabilities and charges	15	(2 466)	(2 418)
Net assets		169 142	157 290
Capital and reserves			
Called up share capital	16	16 313	16 144
Share premium account	17	3 340	2 107
Revaluation reserve	17	60 349	60 017
Profit and loss account	17	89 140	79 022
Amounts attributable to equity interests		169 142	157 290

Extract from notes to the accounts

The following extract from the notes to the accounts of Mansfield Brewery plc explains fixed assets:

Note 10 Tangible assets a) Movement during year	Brewery and other industrial properties £000	Licensed and unlicensed properties £000	Machinery equipment and vehicles £000	Total £000
Cost or valuation:				
At 30 March 1996	14022	183412	57252	254686
Additions	1207	10147	11021	22375
Disposals	(450)	(1775)	(1846)	(4071)
At 29 March 1997	14779	191784	66427	272990
Accumulated depreciation:				
At 30 March 1996	1904	—	32286	34190
Provided in year	399	300	5773	6472
Disposals	—	—	(1481)	(1481)
At 29 March 1997	2303	300	36578	39181
Net book amount				
At 29 March 1997	**12476**	**191484**	**29849**	**233809**
At 30 March 1996	12118	183412	24966	220496

The cost of assets includes an amount of £255 000 in respect of interest capitalised (1996: £122 000).

b) At 29 March 1997	Cost or valuation £000	Depreciation £000	Net book amount £000
Brewery and other industrial properties:			
Freehold	14768	2292	12476
Leasehold under 50 years	11	11	—
Licensed and unlicensed properties:			
Freehold	173194	—	173194
Leasehold over 50 years	9139	—	9139
Leasehold under 50 years	9451	300	9151
Total properties	206563	2603	203960
Machinery, equipment and vehicles at cost	66427	36578	29849
	272990	39181	233809
Cost or valuation of properties comprise:			
Licensed properties revalued in 1996	180114		
Other assets revalued in 1989	7699		
Others stated at cost	18750		
	206563		

Comparable amounts for the revalued properties
under the historical cost convention would be:

At 29 March 1997	**127 464**	**2 688**	**124 776**
At 30 March 1996	129 568	2 083	127 485

The capital value at the date of installation, of plant and equipment leased under finance leases amounted to £3 128 000 (1996: £1 732 000). The accumulated depreciation on these assets was £1 785 000 (1996: £1 680 000).

	1997	1996
	£000	*£000*
c) Future capital expenditure		
Contracted for but not provided for in the accounts	5 293	6 147

▪ Current liabilities

Current liabilities are creditors falling due within one year (£32 534), and they are deducted from current assets in order to calculate *net current assets*, or working capital, in this case a negative figure (£954). Current liabilities include trade creditors awaiting payment for goods and services delivered, accruals, the bank overdraft which is usually reviewed every six months, tax awaiting payment, and dividends declared but not yet paid to shareholders. Usually a note to the accounts gives details of these amounts.

▪ Long term liabilities

The fixed assets plus or minus working capital (£257 253) is an important figure, sometimes termed *net capital employed*, which represents the long-term investment of funds in the business by shareholders and long-term lenders. If long-term liabilities (£85 645), and provisions (£2466) are deducted from net capital employed, the resulting figure (£169 142) represents the net assets of the business, the total assets *less* all borrowings, and thus the shareholders' funds invested in the business.

▪ Shareholders' funds

Shareholders' funds, or equity interest (share capital is sometimes called equity), comprises the nominal value of the share capital issued to holders (£16 313) *plus* all the reserves of the business. The share premium account (£3340) is a capital reserve derived from the surplus generated when shares are issued for more than their face value. The revaluation reserve (£60 349) is the surplus created when assets are revalued and counted in the balance sheet at their new values. This is really a profit, but because valuations are subjective, the surplus does not go through the profit and loss account, but is posted to a reserve instead. It is a profit belonging to the shareholders, and they should be informed, but since it lacks certainty and could be reversed by market changes the amount cannot prudently be distributed as a dividend. The remaining reserve concerns past profit belonging to the shareholders and is retained in the business (£89 140), as a source of funds.

Note that for Mansfield Brewery plc this amount alone exceeds the long-term loans (£85 645). Note also that unappropriated profit at the beginning of the year (£79 022), when added to the retained profit for the year from the profit and loss account (£10 450), gives £89 472, which *less* £332 – a past revaluation of property written back to profit and loss – reconciles to £89 140. Thus the balance sheet is connected to the profit and loss account because the retained profit each year is added to the reserves.

THE FINANCIAL POSITION

The balance sheet shows the book value of the assets controlled by the business, but this may not be a true value for the wealth owned by the shareholders. Some assets are not recorded on the balance sheet since items such as brands and goodwill are often excluded. How, for example, do you value the know-how, skill and morale of the workforce in a company, which is so significant to generate a profit, or the fact that marketing has developed a demand for the product which leads to extra sales? The assets which are recorded may be counted at historical costs, or at a valuation made since their purchase. An aggregate figure for assets which includes some at cost and others at a valuation is not very meaningful. By adding together the book entry for each asset, their enhanced value when combined in the business is disregarded. Perhaps the real value of a business can be found by multiplying the number of shares at issue by the market value for each share. This too is unreliable, however, since the market value is derived from current trading of small blocks of shares, and is therefore likely to be below the price offered by a takeover bidder who is seeking to control the whole business.

If the balance sheet is not a valuation statement, at least it shows the relative importance of the lenders and shareholders who have financed the business, and the manner in which their funds have been invested in assets of various classes. Funds borrowed for a short period are distinguished from funds borrowed for repayment well into the future.

The fact that the balance sheet shows the position at one point in time introduces a further element of caution because it is similar to a photograph of the business – and photographs can be improved if the subject adopts a careful pose. There is no guarantee that the position will not change soon after the balance sheet date, even though Statement of Standard Accounting Practice No. 17 (SSAP 17) requires that post-balance-sheet events which affect the position should be disclosed by a note to the accounts.

MEASURING A TRUE PROFIT

The transactions approach to profit measurement holds that sales for the year minus costs measures profit, so long as the costs are adjusted for accruals and prepayments and matched to the goods sold. Prudence adds a further item to this calculation by providing for future losses derived from current transactions.

There is, however, an alternative approach to profit measurement, which relates accounting to its sister discipline of economics. This approach suggests that if the wealth of the shareholders, when expressed as net assets, has increased during the year for reasons other than increased investment, this increase measures the profit for the year. Under this theory a true surplus can only be identified after amounts have been set aside to maintain the capital of the business, so profit depends on the valuation of the assets at the beginning and end of the year rather than on the traditional transactions approach. This means that the balance sheet is seen as the dominant statement and more important than the traditional profit and loss account, despite the problems associated with valuing the wealth of the business.

Here, then, is a good example of the evolution of accounting principles, as a high-powered argument is being conducted amongst accountants on this point.

The traditionalists argue that the balance sheet is a sheet of balances left after costs and revenues for the year have been transferred to the profit and loss account. This view, however, ignores the significance of the balance sheet as a position statement, showing assets and the sources of finance used to pay for them.

Capital maintenance is an important principle when measuring profit, but the existence of different views as to what is capital and how it should be measured clouds the issue. The valuation approach certainly gives shareholders information about value increases that belong to them but which do not stem from everyday business transactions. However, valuation is subjective, time consuming and expensive, so a complete revaluation of all of the assets in a business could not be undertaken each year. Meanwhile, the financial statements show an awkward intermediate position, as some assets are disclosed at historical cost while other assets appear in the balance sheet at revalued amounts, perhaps derived some years before. The following extension to Note 10 on the fixed assets of Mansfield Brewery plc (see below) illustrates this point, as the company owns considerable property assets:

Note 10 Tangible Assets (*continued*) b) At 29 March 1997	Cost or valuation *£000*	Depreciation *£000*	Net book amount *£000*
Brewery and other industrial properties:			
Freehold	14 768	2 292	12 476
Leasehold under 50 years	11	11	—
Licensed and unlicensed properties:			
Freehold	173 194	—	173 194
Leasehold over 50 years	9 139	—	9 139
Leasehold under 50 years	9 451	300	9 151
Total properties	206 563	2 603	203 960
Machinery, equipment and vehicles at cost	66 427	36 578	29 849
	272 990	39 181	233 809

Cost or valuation of properties comprise:

Licensed properties revalued in 1996	180 114		
Other assets revalued in 1989	7 699		
Others stated at cost	18 750		
	206 563		

Comparable amounts for the revalued properties
under the historical cost convention would be:

At 29 March 1997	**127 464**	**2 688**	**124 776**
At 30 March 1996	129 568	2 083	127 485

The capital value at the date of installation, of plant and equipment leased under finance leases amounted to £3 128 000 (1996: £1 732 000). The accumulated depreciation on these assets was £1 785 000 (1996: £1 680 000).

	1997	1996
	£000	£000
c) Future capital expenditure		
Contracted for but not provided for in the accounts	5 293	6 147

This is a good example of a note which explains a very significant group of assets which are disclosed in the balance sheet by just one figure (£233 809).

CONCLUSION

The profit and loss account and balance sheet present their information in a form prescribed by statute, which is supplemented by notes to the accounts to give detailed explanation of some items. Profit is measured in accordance with the matching principle so accruals and prepayments are necessary to adjust recorded cost to cost incurred. Amounts are provided out of profit to meet costs whose amount is as yet uncertain, and any future losses which might relate to current transactions. Judgement is exercised with prudence in these calculations. Once the profit figure is 'struck', the amount is appropriated for tax, dividend, and retained profit, with some amounts set aside as reserves.

The balance sheet expresses the accounting equation (A – L = C) by setting liabilities against assets. Unfortunately, not all the assets are disclosed, and the mixing of historic costs and values of different dates reduces the reliability and comparability of the amounts.

There is considerable argument among accountants as to how to measure a true profit, and how far a profit derived from transactions should be adjusted for value changes experienced during the year. If capital maintenance is fundamental to profit measurement, an agreed definition of capital and its value is an important prerequisite.

DISCUSSION TOPICS

Thirty-minute essay questions

1 'Judgement is needed to measure a true profit.' – Explain.

2 The balance sheet is arranged to express the accounting equation. Explain with reference to retained profit.

3 'The balance sheet discloses the value of the business.' Discuss.

4 Standard setters are suggesting a change to the way in which profit is measured. Set out their views, and those of the traditionalists who are against change.

PRACTICE QUESTIONS

2.1 Company A has an accounting year which ends on 31 December. The accounting records disclose that:

1 Insurance for the year of £140 000 was paid in advance on 1 July.
2 Rates for the half-year of £50 000 were paid on 1 October.
3 Electricity bills are received quarterly, but only three bills are recorded so far: they are £7800, £6900 and £7200. The bill for the final quarter of the year is expected to be for an average amount of electricity used.
4 Debtors outstanding are £1 320 000, but prudence suggests that 2 per cent of debtors will not pay what they owe.

Required

What adjustments to the profit and loss account are needed for items 1–4 above, and how will those adjustments affect the balance sheet?

2.2 The following balances appear in the accounting records of Aye Shop Ltd:

	£
Sales	750 000
Opening stock	38 000
Purchases	450 000
Administration expenses	97 000
Selling and distribution costs	65 000
Interest	21 000

Administration expenses to be accrued are £20 000, and selling costs paid in advance £5000. The closing stock is counted as £54 000, and tax payable is expected to be £37 000. The company intends to pay a dividend of 15 pence per share on the 400 000, 50-pence shares which are issued.

Required

Draft a profit and loss account for Aye Shop Ltd, in good form, and calculate the earnings per share (EPS).

2.3 Bee Shop Ltd, has been in business for a number of years. Recently there has been a fire in the office where the accounting records are kept, and the records have been destroyed. The directors have asked you to draft a balance sheet as at the date of the fire. You take stock, visit the bank, communicate with customers who have not paid their monthly accounts, and investigate the ownership of buildings, machinery and other assets. You discover the following information:

	£
Cash in the safe	24 000
Bank balance	130 000
Stock	270 000
Debtors	30 000
Shares in other companies	10 000
Land and buildings at a valuation	200 000
Shop fixtures and fittings at a valuation	85 000
Vehicles at a valuation	37 000

After a check of invoices received from suppliers and statements of account you calculate that £75 000 is owed to trade creditors, and £30 000 is owed to the Inland Revenue. The land and buildings are mortgaged in the sum of £170 000. The share register shows that 400 000 £1 shares have been issued.

Required

(a) Draft a balance sheet for Bee Shop Ltd.

(b) Explain how the accounting equation has helped you to complete the balance sheet.

3 Tangible fixed assets and depreciation

OBJECTIVES

The aims of this chapter are to enable students to:

- appreciate the significance of capital expenditure for the measurement of profit;

- understand the reasons for depreciation;

- explain the judgement needed to depreciate fixed assets and the methodology employed;

- apply the main accounting rules for depreciation; and

- operate a simple management system to control fixed assets.

CAPITAL EXPENDITURE

Capital expenditure is the investment of business funds in fixed assets that are intended to make a contribution to profit in more than one accounting year. The profit figure would be distorted if the cost of a machine with a five-year economic life was written off to profit and loss account in Year 1, allowing the following four years a 'free ride'. It is fairer to capitalise the cost of the machine and treat it as an asset in the balance sheet, so that depreciation can spread the cost over the five-year period. Thus capital expenditure relieves the profit and loss account of the cost of the asset in the first year of life, but charges that year a proportion of the cost as depreciation. Some managers may argue for capitalisation of non-capital expenditure in order to improve profit in the current year, so rules for capitalisation have been developed.

Capital expenditure is money spent to purchase or add to the value of fixed assets, to extend or improve the tasks which they can perform, and thus increase their earning capacity. Revenue expenditure that is charged in the profit and loss account concerns money spent in the normal course of the business to operate or maintain the earning capacity of the capital assets. The amount that can be capitalised includes the cost of the machine, delivery expenses, legal costs associated with the purchase, inspection, demolition to make way for a new machine, the construction of foundations and so forth, and the cost of training staff to operate the new machine. In some instances a business will use its own labour force to install machinery, and this cost should also be capitalised. The cost of bringing a second-hand machine to working condition is part of the capital cost of that machine. Later expenditure to reduce running costs or increase the range of operations of a machine can also be capitalised – repairs must be treated differently from improvements. In the case of a new building or a factory which may take several years to complete, the cost of interest on funds borrowed to finance the asset can be capitalised as part of the cost of the asset. Mansfield Brewery plc capitalised £255 000 of such interest in 1997 (see Note 10 to the accounts in the last chapter page 19).

TASK 3.1   A company is reorganising its computing facilities, and the following costs have been incurred. Make a reasoned judgement to allocate the costs as capital or revenue items:

		£
(a)	Cost of new terminals	75 000
(b)	Cost of new software	45 000
(c)	Servicing and repairs to printers	25 000
(d)	Cost of redecorating the computer room	12 000
(e)	Training staff to use new hardware	17 000
(f)	New attachment for printers to extend the colour range and typeface available	4 000

Solution

Judgement must be applied to consider the cost of acquiring, extending or improving the assets. Only items (c) and (d) concern maintenance.

DEPRECIATION

■ Rationale and theory

To an economist, depreciation is a matter of valuation, because as a fixed asset ages, its value falls. The fall in value is the result of physical wear and tear, the passage of time with a lease, or obsolescence. As the value of a machine is reduced because technical advances bring new and more efficient machines to compete, or because demand falls for the product of the machine, it is said to be obsolescent. The fall in value in a year is the cost of holding the machine for that year which should be charged to the profit and loss account.

To an accountant, less willing to rely on valuation, depreciation is a matter of allocation, as the cost of the asset is spread over the years of its useful economic life in order to measure a true profit each year. A management accountant might consider depreciation to be the amount which must be charged to a department for the use of the machine, perhaps on a monthly or even hourly rate. So depreciation is significant for profit measurement under the matching concept.

Alternatively, depreciation is important as a means whereby capital is maintained. It is the amount set aside out of profit to replace funds tied up in the asset which have been used up during the year. This is not a savings scheme for the replacement of the asset, since machines are rarely replaced by the same thing, because over time, technological advances bring change. Depreciation will ensure that the capital invested in the business is replaced out of profit as the asset financed by that capital is used up.

EXAMPLE John wins £40 000 on the lottery, and uses the money to purchase an articulated truck since he wants to go into business as a long-haul lorry driver. His balance sheet on 1 January 19x1 shows capital invested £40 000 and assets £40 000. The vehicle is expected to have a working life of eight years, so depreciation will be £40 000 ÷ 8 = £5000 each year.

During the first year John has receipts of £200 000 and costs of £180 000. His profit and loss account shows:

	£	
Sales revenue	200 000	(received in cash)
Costs	180 000	(paid in cash)
Surplus	20 000	(cash balance)
Depreciation	5 000	
Profit	15 000	(all paid out as dividend)

John's balance sheet at the end of Year 1 will be:

	£
Fixed asset	40 000
less Depreciation	5 000
Net book value	35 000
Cash (£20 000 – £15 000)	5 000
Net assets	40 000
Capital	40 000

After eight years of trading, assuming the profit and loss account is the same each year, the balance sheet will disclose:

	£
Fixed asset at cost	40 000
less Depreciation to date	40 000
Net book value (the lorry is now worthless)	nil
Cash (£5000 × 8)	40 000
Net assets	40 000
Capital	40 000

John's capital has been maintained because he has the same amount of cash as at the start of his business. Profit was reduced each year by the provision for depreciation, which reduced the profit available for dividend. If no depreciation had been charged against profit John would have spent his supposed profit of £20 000 each year, and would have had no cash at all at the end of Year 8. John can now decide on his future business policy: he can purchase a new vehicle, or go into some other business, or retire – his capital is intact. One problem, however, is that the depreciation was based on historical cost, and has maintained the capital sum in money terms *but not* the purchasing power of that sum. After eight years of inflation, even at 2.5 per cent per annum, John will not be able to purchase a replacement vehicle for £40 000.

■ The methodology

Depreciation depends on judgement to estimate at the beginning of an asset's life the length of life and the scrap value (residual value) of the asset, if any, at the end of that life. Estimates are often wrong! It is the responsibility of the directors to select a method of depreciation which is most appropriate for the company concerned. Several methods are available for selection.

The straight-line method

This method is widely used in practice being simple to operate. The cost of the asset less the residual value is divided by the years of life of the asset in order to give an equal charge for depreciation each year:

$$\frac{\text{cost} - \text{residual value}}{\text{useful economic life}} = \text{annual depreciation}$$

TASK 3.2

A new machine is purchased for £80 000, with delivery charges £1000, and provision of foundations by the company's own labour £4000. The machinery is estimated to have a useful economic life of five years, and a residual value of £5000. How would this machine appear in the balance sheet at the end of the second year of its life and at the end of Year 5, using the straight-line method of depreciation?

Solution

(Cost – residual value) ÷ life
(£85 000 – £5000) ÷ 5 = £16 000 per year

		£	
Year 2 Balance sheet entry	Machine at cost	85 000	
	less depreciation to date	32 000	(£16 000 × 2)
	Net book value	53 000	
Year 5 Balance sheet entry	Machine at cost	85 000	
	less Depreciation to date	80 000	(£16 000 × 5)
	Equal to scrap value	5 000	

The reducing-balance method

This method writes off the same percentage each year from an ever-decreasing balance. For example, a machine costing £80 000 with a percentage write-off rate of 15 per cent would be depreciated as follows:

Cost	80 000	
Depreciation Year 1 (£80 000 × 0.15)	*12 000	(profit and loss)
Remaining balance	68 000	(balance sheet)
Depreciation Year 2 (£68 000 × 0.15)	*10 200	
Remaining balance	57 800	
Depreciation Year 3 £57 800 × 0.15)	*8 670	
Remaining balance	49 130	

The calculation continues until the asset reaches the end of its life, when the remaining balance is written off to profit and loss, net of any cash received for the scrap value of the machine.

*This method charges more depreciation in early years and less in later years (see asterisked amounts) to compensate for heavy repair bills, but this may distort the true cost of using the machine and adversely affect replacement decisions. It is possible to use a mathematical formula to calculate the rate to apply to each situation of cost, residual value and life, but this is never used in practice, as a rate is arbitrarily selected and applied to a group of similar assets.

The machine hour method

With this method, cost less residual value is divided by the estimated number of hours the machine will work throughout its life. This gives an hourly rate which can be applied to the hours worked by the machine during a month or a year, as the charge for depreciation. This method relates the charge in the profit and loss account to usage of the machine rather than the passage of time.

TASK 3.3

A machine is purchased for £85 000 with an estimated residual value of £5000. The machine has an estimated working life of 20 000 hours. In Year 1 it works 3000 hours and in Year 2 it works for 8000 hours. Calculate the depreciation charge for Years 1 and 2, and the balance sheet entry for the machine at the end of Year 2.

Solution

(£85 000 – £5000) ÷ 20 000 hours = £4 per hour

£

Year 1 3000 hours x £4 = 12 000 depreciation
Year 2 8000 hours x £4 = 32 000 depreciation

Balance sheet at end of Year 2		
	Plant at cost	85 000
	less Depreciation to date	44 000
	Net book value	41 000

But what happens if the machine is not used in Year 3 and falls in value due to obsolescence? Because depreciation is now a matter of system, further checks and rules are needed to account for changes when estimates are later proved to be wrong.

■ Extra rules for special situations

Statement of Standard Accounting Practice No. 12 (SSAP 12) contains some extra rules for application when the estimates built in to depreciation calculations prove to be wrong. In practice, managers select the method they wish to use and apply it consistently as a matter of accounting policy. Assets are grouped together and a standard life is applied to the group or a percentage is arbitrarily selected for the reducing-balance method. When an asset is scrapped or sold, the difference between its book value and the cash received is written off to the profit and loss account. Land is not depreciated, so with property the cost must be analysed between the land and the building on the land, and the building cost only is subject to depreciation.

Financial Reporting Exposure Draft 17 (FRED 17) will soon replace SSAP 12, but the rules shown below will probably be adopted by this new standard.

1 *Changes in value during the life of the asset.* If an asset – say, a building – increases in value during its working life, the new value should be shown in the balance sheet, and the difference between the old net book value and the new value shown as a *revaluation reserve* in the balance sheet. The new value is depreciated over the remaining years of the asset's life. If the asset subsequently falls in value, the deficit is written off, first against the revaluation reserve for that asset, and if that is not enough, then the remainder is written off to the profit and loss account. Once again the new value is depreciated over the remaining years of the asset's life.

2 *Extension of the life expectancy of the asset.* If a machine bought in 19x1 with an expected life of five years, is reviewed in Year 3 (19x3) and found to have an expected life of six more years at that point, the net book value at Year 3 is depreciated over the next six years. The asset would usually also be revalued at this point where its life changes.

3 *Additional expenditure.* If, part way through its life, extra fitments are added to a machine, this extra capital expenditure is added to the net book value and depreciated over the remaining life of the asset.

4 *Premature retirement.* If a machine with an eight-year life is found to be obsolete and worthless at the end of four years, the book value at that point is written off to the profit and loss account. Depreciation over the last four years has been insufficient, and profit in those years has been overstated, so this error of judgement must be set right at once.

5 *Assets which work on.* If a machine which is expected to have a life of five years is still able to work at the end of that period, it should then be revalued and the new value depreciated over the further expected life of the asset. The revaluation surplus is posted to a revaluation reserve.

EXAMPLE A company purchased a complex item of plant for £950 000 on 1 January 1996. The plant was expected to have a life of seven years, and a residual value of

£40 000 when taken out of service on 31 December 2002. The following events have been aranged to take place every two years:

- On 1 January 1998 an extension to the machine was purchased for £75 000. The life and scrap value of the machine was not affected by this item.
- On 1 January 2000 the life of the machine was reviewed and it was expected to continue to operate until 31 December 2009, but with no scrap value.
- On 1 January 2002 the machine underwent a major overhaul costing £20 000, and, as a result, was revalued at £440 000. Life expectancy remained the same, with no scrap value.
- On 1 January 2004 the machine was considered to be obsolete and it was sold for £200 000.

Required

You are required to calculate and explain the amounts of depreciation charged to the profit and loss account in respect of this machine for the years 1996 to 2003.

Solution

	£
Cost of asset	950 000
less Depreciation 1996 + 1997 [((950 – 40) ÷ 7) × 2]	260 000
Net book value at 31 December 1997	690 000
plus Extra investment at 1 January 1998 (add to net book value)	75 000
Net book value at 1 January 1998	765 000
less Depreciation 1998 + 1999 (765 – 40 ÷ 5 × 2) (recalculate depreciation)	290 000
Net book value at 1 January 2000	475 000
less Depreciation 2000 + 2001 (475 ÷ 10 × 2) (life extended/no scrap value)	95 000
Net book value at 1 January 2002 (overhaul not capitalised)	380 000
Revaluation reserve (plant brought up to new value)	60 000*
New value	440 000
less Depreciation 2002 + 2003 (440 ÷ 8 × 2) (depreciation recalculated)	110 000
	330 000
Sold 1 January 2004	200 000
Deficit	130 000
less Transfer from revaluation reserve	60 000*
Loss written off to profit and loss account	£70 000

CONTROLLING FIXED ASSETS

Control is facilitated if appropriate information is provided for managers. Most businesses will own a number of fixed assets and in large organisations the control of this significant investment is vital to efficient operation. Management will need to be aware of the following information:

(a) the location of each asset;

(b) the extent to which it is being used or lying idle;

(c) the repairs which have been carried out on the asset and the cost of those repairs;

(d) the expiry dates of any licences permitting the organisation to use the asset;

(e) the cost of using the asset (e.g. running costs, wastage, breakdowns, etc.).

In addition, for management purposes further information is required as follows:

(f) the date of purchase;

(g) the name and address of the asset's supplier; availability of spares;

(h) the cost of asset; the date and amount of any additions to the asset;

(i) the estimated useful economic life of the asset; when the life was last reviewed;

(j) the estimated scrap or resale value of the asset at the end of its useful economic life;

(k) a description of the asset;

(l) a code number for the asset so that it can be found easily on a computerised system;

(m) the method of depreciation to be used for the asset;

(n) the accumulated depreciation of the asset; the net book value;

(o) details of the disposal of the asset when it has occurred;

(p) date and cost of last major overhaul;

(q) revaluation: date, amount, valuer.

This information is normally recorded in a fixed asset register. The efficiency of the organisation can be greatly improved if the register is stored on a computer. Specialist computer packages exist for the recording of an organisation's fixed assets, but much the same effect can be obtained by using a database programme, particularly in smaller organisations or where the information is recorded within each department.

In the context of a fixed asset register, each asset would be given a code number. There would be a separate record on the computer file for each fixed asset, and within each record there would be a field for each data item to be recorded. The asset code would normally be used as the key field so that the record of any particular asset could be located easily.

The use of a computerised fixed asset register would allow the calculation of depreciation to be automated and various managerial reports could be produced showing, for example:

■ the depreciation charge for the accounting period analysed by asset and by department as required;

■ a list of assets requiring servicing;

■ a list of assets at a particular location;

■ the extent of any repair expenditure on each asset;

■ a list of assets continuing in use beyond their estimated useful economic life.

CONCLUSION

Capital expenditure is a significant item for every business, because it concerns the long-lived assets such as plant, buildings and vehicles, which are used to earn the profit. Expenditure that is capitalised is not charged to the profit and loss account in the year in which the money is spent, but spread over the economic life of the acquired asset by a provision for depreciation. Depreciation is significant for the measurement of a true profit, and also to maintain the capital invested in the business.

Considerable judgement is required to calculate depreciation since the life span of the asset and its residual value are uncertain at the date of acquisition. There are several different methods whereby depreciation can spread the cost over the life of the asset but it is the responsibility of the board to select an appropriate method and use it consistently as an accounting policy. Assets are usually grouped together, and an arbitrary life applied to that group. Mansfield Brewery plc depreciates plant and equipment at rates varying from 3 per cent to 30 per cent. When setting the rate, the effect of obsolescence on the life of the asset must be considered.

Such an important item as fixed assets must be controlled by managers, with a system designed to disclose information which will assist in that control process.

DISCUSSION TOPICS

Thirty-minute essay questions

1 'The recognition of capital expenditure is significant for profit measurement.' Discuss.

2 Explain, with an example, the relationship between depreciation and the maintenance of capital.

3 Explain the rules which have been developed to overcome the effect of uncertainty on depreciation calculations.

4 You are to attend a managerial meeting to discuss the control of tangible fixed assets. In preparation for this meeting, list and justify ten items of information which would be helpful to managers when control of machinery is discussed.

PRACTICE QUESTIONS

3.1 Bee Ltd depreciates plant using the straight-line method and an eight-year life. A machine was bought for £50 000 in 1992 and it was estimated to have a residual value of £6000. The machine was sold for £12 000 in 1997.

Required

Calculate the charge for depreciation in each year of the life of the machine.

3.2 Cee Ltd purchased a machine for £40 000 in 1992, and intended to use it for five years by which time it would be worthless.

Required

Calculate the charge for each year of the life of the machine using (a) the straight-line method and (b) the reducing-balance method with a 30 per cent rate.

3.3 **(a)** ABC Ltd is a medium-sized manufacturing business. The production manager is a qualified mechanical and electrical engineer. At a recent management meeting he commented as follows: 'I cannot understand the need to charge depreciation against profit. The cash has already been spent to buy the machine so all we need to do is save up for a replacement'.

Required

Draft a brief memorandum to the production manager to explain the concept of depreciation.

(b) **(i)** ABC Ltd invested £750 000 in a complex piece of plant on 1 January 1994. This machinery was expected to have a life of eight years and a residual value of £30 000 when taken out of service on 31 December 2001.

(ii) On 1 January 1996 the machine was fitted with a new attachment which increased the range of operations it could perform. This attachment cost £60 000.

(iii) On 1 January 1997 the machine was revalued at £640 000 and was expected to continue in operation until 31 December 2004 when it would be worthless.

(iv) The machine was sold for £250 000 on 31st December 1999.

Required

Calculate and explain the amounts of depreciation charged to the profit and loss account in respect of this machine for the years 1994 to 1999 using the straight-line method.

4 The accounting treatment of stocks and debtors

OBJECTIVES

The aims of this chapter are to enable students to:

- appreciate the significance of stock valuation for the measurement of profit;
- understand the terms 'cost' and 'net realisable value';
- explain the implications of the cost flow assumption;
- calculate stock values and profits based on FIFO, LIFO and AVCO; and
- account for doubtful debts, bad debts and bad debts later paid.

THE SIGNIFICANCE OF STOCK FOR PROFIT MEASUREMENT

The term 'stock' covers five categories:

1 raw materials and components – waiting to be used in the factory;
2 products at an intermediate stage of completion – work in progress, partly finished;
3 finished goods awaiting sale;
4 consumable stores – fuel, oil, grease and other items to be used up in production; and
5 goods purchased for resale in a retail situation.

Stock is important in the calculation 'opening stock *plus* purchases *less* closing stock', which computes the cost of goods sold or manufactured (*see* page 15). Therefore, the valuation placed on opening and closing stocks will directly influence the measurement of profit. SSAP 9 *Stocks and long-term contracts* contains detailed rules as to the accounting treatment of this important current asset. This standard has caused great difficulty in practice since it seeks to ban certain stock valuation methods which have long been used by companies, and in some respects the rules in the standard are in conflict with the Companies Act 1985.

Profit measurement requires that costs and related revenues should be matched together. Part of this matching exercise concerns the identification of the cost of unsold or unconsumed stock and work in progress, at the end of a period which must be carried forward as an asset at the end of that period, to be charged as a cost against future revenue. The valuation put upon closing stock will influence the amount of the cost charged in the current period, and the amount carried forward to be charged in the next period. Thus the accounting treatment of stock is important for matching, for profit measurement, and for the valuation of assets in the balance sheet. An error in the valuation of stock will distort the profit made in the current year, and in the next year as well.

THE BASIC RULE FOR THE VALUATION OF STOCK

The cost allocated to stock should comprise expenditure incurred in the normal course of business to bring the stock to its present location and condition, including all related production overheads. The method chosen to allocate costs to stock should provide a fair approximation to the expenditure actually incurred on the stock. The basic rule is that stock should be carried in the accounts at 'the lower of cost and net realisable value'. This rule is part of the concept of prudence.

If an item of stock has a net realisable value greater than its cost, it is accounted for at cost and the surplus is not considered to be a profit. Yet if an item of stock has a net realisable value which is less than its cost, then the consequent loss made but not yet realised is recognised at once in the profit and loss account. The comparison of cost and net realisable value should be made for each item of stock, but where this is impracticable, similar stock items can be grouped together for this purpose. It is considered unacceptable to compare the total net realisable value of all stock with the total cost of all the stock, because this would net off foreseeable losses that must be recognised in the profit computation against unrealised profits which are not to be recognised.

WHAT IS COST?

Cost in relation to stocks of raw material includes the cost of purchase (which is the price, *plus* import duties) transport and handling costs and any other attributable costs, *less* trade discounts, rebates and subsidies. The cost of stocks of work in progress or finished goods includes the cost of material used and the cost of conversion, which comprises:

1 costs specifically attributable to stock items such as direct labour and direct expenses or subcontract work;
2 production overheads incurred to provide production services. An appropriate proportion of such overheads should be added to the direct costs of stock, but the overheads should be based on the normal level of activity, taking one year with another. Overheads should be classified according to function such as production, selling or administration, so that conversion costs include production overheads (e.g. depreciation) but exclude administration or selling costs. (Note that there is some argument among accountants as to whether it is truly match-

ing to carry part of production overheads of one year to set off against sales in the next year.)

The proportion of total overheads charged to stock, and therefore carried forward into the next accounting period, should be based on *normal* levels of production. Abnormal conversion costs such as exceptionable spoilage, idle capacity, and so forth, concern the current year, and should therefore be charged against profits in that year rather than carried forward in the cost of stock. This is in accordance with the matching concept.

Overheads relating to marketing and selling costs cannot be carried forward in the cost of work in progress or finished goods stock since they relate to items which have been sold already, but if a firm sales contract exists for the provision of goods, then it is fair to assume that these costs have been incurred in part to win that contract. Accordingly, under these special circumstances, marketing and selling costs can form part of the overheads charged against stock.

General management overheads are not normally directly related to production and are thus excluded from overheads in the cost of stock carried forward. The cost of a central service department (e.g. the computer department, typing pool or the accounts department itself) may, in part, serve the production function. Only those costs of service departments which can be reasonably allocated to production can be included as part of the cost of conversion of stock to work in progress or finished goods stock.

It is not considered conservative or prudent to value stocks without including their proportion of the production overheads. Prudence can be injected into the calculation in the determination of the net realisable value.

EXAMPLE

FAB Furniture plc makes coffee tables.

- Each item takes 5 kilos of raw material at £3 per kilo, plus three hours of labour at £6 per hour, plus two hours of machine time at £2 per hour to produce one coffee table.
- Packaging costs are £2 per unit, with one hour of labour to check and pack each unit before it is dispatched to customers.
- Annual overhead costs are budgeted to be:

	£
Production	190 000
Design	10 000
Transport	30 000
Selling	40 000
Administration	70 000

- The factory overheads include exceptional spoilage of £4000 and abnormal idle time of £8000.
- The administration costs include the cost of the accounts department of £20 000, 10 per cent of which is incurred in costing the production function.

■ The factory is designed to produce 50 000 units a year, but this year the budget is set at 45 000 units. There are 3000 coffee tables in stock.

Stock valuation

Overheads

	£	£
Production overhead		190 000
less		
Abnormal idle time	8 000	
Exceptional spoilage	4 000	
		12 000
		178 000
add Office cost (10% of £20 000)		2 000
Normal annual overhead costs		180 000

Divide by normal budget production of 45 000 units to find a cost per unit:

£180 000 ÷ 45 000 = £4 per unit

Cost of finished goods stock

	£
Direct costs:	
materials (5 kilos at £3)	15
labour (3 hours at £6)	18
machining (2 hours at £2)	4
	37
Overheads per unit	4
	41

3000 units × £41 = £123 000

Packaging costs do not concern unpacked items in stock.

WHAT IS NET REALISABLE VALUE (NRV)?

NRV is defined as the actual or estimated selling price of stock less trade discounts net of all further costs to complete production of the stock and all costs to be incurred to market, sell or distribute the stock.

If the NRV of a stock item is less than its cost, an amount equal to the deficit must be provided out of profit and set off against the cost of stock in the balance sheet. NRV is likely to be less than cost when:

■ costs are increasing or selling prices are falling;
■ there is physical deterioration of stocks;
■ products are becoming obsolete, which means that sales are slowing down and stocks may not be cleared;
■ marketing strategy determines to sell certain products for less than their costs (a loss leader);

■ mistakes are made in production or purchasing which overstock the stores or accumulate spoiled items in the warehouse.

EXAMPLE The facts are as for FAB Furniture plc in the example above, plus:

■ The selling price per coffee table is £50.
■ A trade discount of 15 per cent is allowed to retailers.

Stock valuation
Selling price *less* the costs to bring the stock to a saleable condition.

	£
Selling price	50.00
less Trade discount (15%)	7.50
	42.50
less Packaging costs of (£2 + labour £6)	8.00
	34.50

Overhead

	£
Administration(70 000 – 2 000 for production accounting)	68 000
Design	10 000
Transport	30 000
Selling	40 000
	148 000
£148 000 ÷ 45 000 units = £3.29 per unit	3.29
Net realisable value per unit	31.21

	£
NRV (3000 units at £31.21)	93 630
Cost (3000 units at £41)	123 000
Amount of provision	£29 370

NRV per unit =

The stock must be written down by £29 370 because NRV is less than the cost. When the 3000 units are sold the revenue less cost of sales will show a loss and it is prudent to provide for that loss now.

BASES OF VALUATION FOR STOCK

■ The cost flow assumption

Normally, raw material stocks are purchased in a series of transactions throughout the year. It is unlikely that each purchase will be at the same price, and it is often difficult to separate raw materials purchased at one price from a later delivery pur-

chased at another price. Accordingly, when stock is taken at the end of the year, the physical quantity can be accurately counted but it is often impossible to work out the price at which individual units of stock were purchased. Liquids from several different deliveries may be mixed in a tank, or building materials or components from separate deliveries mixed together in a store. It is necessary, therefore to make a 'cost flow assumption' to determine whether the items remaining in stock at the end of the period are deemed to come from the batch most recently purchased or from the batch purchased at the beginning of the period. If separate purchases are at different prices, the cost flow assumption will influence the profit disclosed, especially in a period of inflation when prices rise steadily. The cost flow assumption is a matter of accounting policy. SSAP 9 suggests that management must exercise judgement when selecting a method to provide a fair practical approximation to actual cost.

■ FIFO, LIFO and AVCO

SSAP 9 favours stock valuation by the unit cost, average cost or FIFO methods. The unit cost method identifies individual units of stock and can price each item at its original cost. Such an identification is rare in practice. The average cost method (AVCO) calculates a weighted average price for all purchases throughout the period and values the stock left at the end of the period according to the average. The FIFO (first in, first out) method assumes that material stocks will be used up in chronological order corresponding to their purchase. This means that the first items delivered will be used up first. Therefore, those remaining at the end of the period will be part of the most recent delivery and should thus be priced at the most recent price paid for the materials. The LIFO (last in, first out) method assumes that material stocks are issued to production on the basis of the most recently received batches used up first. Hence closing stock is assumed to be drawn from batches purchased earlier in the period and the charge for materials used will be based on more recent prices.

FIFO

With FIFO, it is a logical assumption that materials are used up in the order in which they were purchased. If prices have risen steadily throughout the accounting period, the early batches of materials purchased will be the cheapest, and it is those batches which are charged against revenue in the profit and loss account. Accordingly, under FIFO there is a tendency to overstate the profit in a period of inflation. It is unfair to tax companies on this overstated profit. The balance sheet valuation of the stock will be true and fair since it is priced at the most recent prices paid for the material.

LIFO

Under LIFO, the charge for the use of raw materials will be at more recent prices, while the stocks remaining at the balance sheet date will be priced at an outdated cost paid for batches received at some time in the past. The profit figure measured